CAN YOU FIND MY LOVE?

IN THE SEA

JAN MARQUART

www.CanYouFindMyLove.com

ISBN: 0996854169
ISBN-13: 9780996854160

Cover and Interior by Publish Pros
www.publishpros.com

Books currently available in the "Can You Find My Love?" Series

Other Books by Jan Marquart

FOR ADULTS

Write to Heal

The Mindful Writer, Still the Mind, Free the Pen

The Basket Weaver, a Novel

Kate's Way, a Novel

Echoes from the Womb, a Book for Daughters

Voices from the Land

The Breath of Dawn, a Journey of Everyday Blessings

How to Write From Your Heart (booklet)

How to Write Your Own Memoir (booklet)

A Manual on How to Deal With a Bully in the Workplace

Cracked Open, a Book of Poems

A Writer's Wisdom

To:

paste
photo
here

_____

NAME

My appreciation to Rich Carnahan, who worked
tirelessly editing the details and photos for this book.
And to master Aiden, who gave valuable reactions to this book,
I send love and hugs. Thank you!

CAN YOU FIND MY LOVE?
is dedicated to all children.

May each child be filled
with love and the fun for learning.

You have received this book
because someone loves you.

Look closely—you will find love hidden
in everyday things that you might
normally take for granted.

This is what it looks like.

♥

When you find the love I have placed
for you, I hope that it warms your
heart and lets you know how
very special you are.

The SEA holds many wonders.

IN THE SEA

FISh

Fins on their tops, bottoms, sides and tails
help fish swim very fast.

SEAHORSES

A seahorse moves through the water
by flicking its tail.

STARFISH

Starfish, or sea stars, move around using the hundreds of tiny feet under each arm.

CAN YOU FIND MY LOVE?

OCTOPUSES

An octopus has eight legs and can change its color to blend into its surroundings.

CAN YOU FIND MY LOVE?

JELLYFISH

Jellyfish look like floating umbrellas and are often see-through or brightly colored.

CAN YOU FIND MY LOVE?

TURTLES

Every 4 to 7 hours, sea turtles have to come to the surface for more air.

CAN YOU FIND MY LOVE?

SAND DOLLARS

A sand dollar may look like a shell,
but it has a fish living inside.

CAN YOU FIND MY LOVE?

ShARKS

Sharks have fifteen rows of teeth and have
been around since before the dinosaurs.

WHALES

Whales are the largest animals in the ocean
and the loudest in the world.

CAN YOU FIND MY LOVE?

SEA LIONS

A sea lion's super-sensitive whiskers
help it find food floating nearby.

DOLPHINS

Dolphins whistle, squeak, click and moan
to talk to one another.

CAN YOU FIND MY LOVE?

ShRIMP

Shrimp can only swim backwards
and are almost colorless in the wild.

CAN YOU FIND MY LOVE?

WALRUSES

Walruses have large teeth, called tusks, that
are used for protection and cutting ice.

CORALS

Although coral may look like a plant, it isn't.
It is a tiny animal called a polyp.

LOBSTERS

Lobsters have two different size claws—one
for pinching and one for crushing.

hERMIT CRABS

These crabs carry and live in shells
left behind by sea snails.

CAN YOU FIND MY LOVE?

SUNKEN SHIPS

Shipwrecks provide "treasures" on the ocean
floor, just waiting to be discovered.

CAN YOU FIND MY LOVE?

EELS

An eel looks like a snake but is actually a fish that lives in caves and between rocks.

STINGRAYS

A stingray's mouth is under its flat body,
so it can eat food off the ocean floor.

CAN YOU FIND MY LOVE?

ANEMONES

Sea anemones look like beautiful flowers
but, like coral, are actually animals.

MANATEES

Manatees, sometimes called sea cows, move
very slowly and look like giant floating rocks.

Did you look close enough
to find all my love?

Can you **DRAW** a few other things found **IN ThE SEA**?

Can you **DRAW** a few other things found **IN THE SEA**?

Can you **DRAW** a few other things found **IN ThE SEA**?

From:

paste
photo
here

_____

NAME

About the Author

Jan Marquart is a psychotherapist and author. She has published 11 books for adults and has had articles, stories, poems and essays published in various newspapers, journals and magazines across the United States, Australia and Europe. She teaches writing for those over fifty and has taught a dozen writing workshops for Story Circle Network.

Jan has designed a 6-week writing course titled *Unveil the Wounded Self - Write to Heal* which focuses on healing PTSD and has also designed a 6-week writing course titled *The Provocation of Journal Writing* to encourage everyone to write their personal stories. She is currently on her 100th daily journal.

Jan can be contacted at JanMarquart.com, JanMarquartlcsw.wordpress.com and at her personal email address, jan@canyoufindmylove.com.

Her books can be purchased from all major online book retailers.

www.ingramcontent.com/pod-product-compliance
Lightning Source LLC
Chambersburg PA
CBHW040248100426
42811CB00011B/1188